My Favorite Bear

P9-CAU-578

Andrea Gabriel

My Favorite Bear

Developmental Studies Center

This book is dedicated with the utmost love and
admiration to my grandmother, Sally Haase—
one of my favorite mama bears.
— A. G.

2004 First paperback edition
Text and illustrations copyright © 2003 by Andrea Gabriel
All rights reserved, including the right of reproduction in whole or in part in any form.
Originally published by Charlesbridge.

For permissions queries contact Charlesbridge,
85 Main Street, Watertown, MA 02472.
(617) 926-0329 www.charlesbridge.com

This Developmental Studies Center edition is published by arrangement with Charlesbridge.

Display and text type set in Jimbo and Garamond No. 3

Developmental Studies Center
1250 53rd Street, Suite 3
Emeryville, CA 94608-2965
800.666.7270 * fax: 510.464.3670
devstu.org

ISBN 978-1-61003-310-7
Printed in China

3 4 5 6 7 8 9 10 RRD 20 19 18 17 16 15

You're my little bear.

One day you'll be grown.

5

You'll meet other bears

when you travel from home.

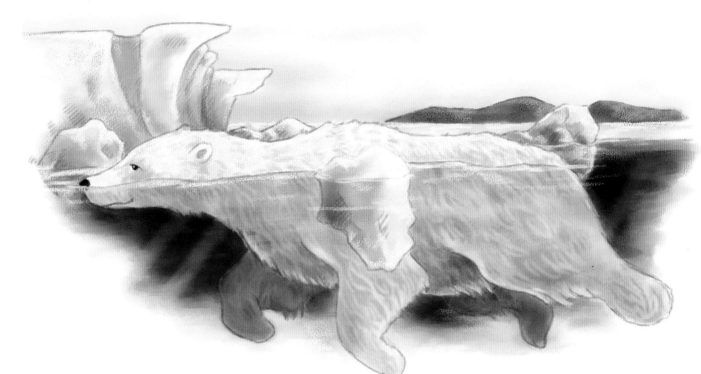

There are bears who like swimming

and bears climbing high,

bears eating berries,

and bears in the sky.

Some bears eat fish.

Some like bamboo.

15

Some bears hunt by
the light of the moon.

There are shy bears,
sticky bears,

and bears feeling lazy,

white bears,

black bears,

21

and bears sniffing daisies.

I'm glad there are bears
of all shapes and all types.

But my favorite bear—
the one who's just right...

. . . is my own sleepy cub.

I love you.
Good night.

Bear Facts

American Black Bear (*Ursus americanus*) Despite its name, the American black bear can be found in a variety of colors: cinnamon, pale blue, white, or brown. Black bears live in forests throughout Canada, the United States, and northern Mexico.

Brown Bear (*Ursus arctos*) The brown bear can be recognized by its shoulder hump and long front claws. Populations of brown bears are found in mountain, tundra, and forested areas of North America, Asia, and Europe.

Polar Bear (*Ursus maritimus*) Many of these bears live most of their lives on the ice, rarely setting foot on land. Polar bears are excellent swimmers, with large paws that propel them through the water. These bears are found throughout the polar regions, and live mostly on a diet of seals.

Asiatic Black Bear (*Ursus thibetanus*) The Asiatic black bear is believed to be a close relative of the American black bear. Asiatic bears have large rounded ears and a V-shaped white patch on their chests. They live in the forests, hills, and mountains of Asia and eat fruit, honey, insects, and carrion.

Sloth Bear (*Melursus ursinus*) The sloth bear is found in the forests and grasslands in and around India. Adapted to a diet of termites and other insects, the sloth bear uses its flexible snout to "vacuum" up its dinner. These bears carry their cubs on their backs, and can be quite aggressive when startled.

Giant Panda (*Ailuropoda melanoleuca*) The giant panda may be the most famous of all endangered species. Only about 1,000 of these bears remain in the wild, living in several mountain areas of China. Pandas mainly eat plants, chiefly bamboo.

Sun Bear (*Helarctos malayanus*) The sun bear is the smallest species of bear, some weighing only 60 pounds when full grown. They are found in the tropical rainforests of Southeast Asia, and live mostly on a diet of plants, insects, and bees' nests.

Spectacled Bear (*Tremarctos ornatus*) The spectacled bear gets its name from the distinctive mask on its face. It is the only species of bear to live in South America. It spends a great deal of time in the trees, and will sometimes build a "nest" for sleeping.